D1074645

# THE BERMUDA TRIANGLE

BY RAY McCLELLAN

BELLWETHER MEDIA • MINNEAPOLIS, MN

Hampshire County

6/2015

**EPIC BOOKS** are no ordinary books. They burst with intense action, high-speed heroics, and shadows of the unknown. Are you ready for an Epic adventure?

This edition first published in 2014 by Bellwether Media, Inc.

No part of this publication may be reproduced in whole or in part without written permission of the publisher. For information regarding permission, write to Bellwether Media, Inc., Attention: Permissions Department, 5357 Penn Avenue South, Minneapolis, MN 55419.

Library of Congress Cataloging-in-Publication Data

McClellan, Ray.
  The Bermuda Triangle / by Ray McClellan.
       pages cm. – (Epic: Unexplained Mysteries)
  Summary: "Engaging images accompany information about the Bermuda Triangle. The combination of high-interest subject matter and light text is intended for students in grades 2 through 7"– Provided by publisher.
  Audience: Ages 7-12.
  Includes bibliographical references and index.
  ISBN 978-1-62617-102-2 (hardcover : alk. paper)
  1.  Shipwrecks–Bermuda Triangle–Juvenile literature. 2.  Bermuda Triangle–Juvenile literature.  I. Title.
  G558.M44 2014
  001.94–dc23
                          2013035914

Text copyright © 2014 by Bellwether Media, Inc. EPIC and associated logos are trademarks and/or registered trademarks of Bellwether Media, Inc. SCHOLASTIC, CHILDREN'S PRESS, and associated logos are trademarks and/or registered trademarks of Scholastic Inc.

Designed by Jon Eppard.

Printed in the United States of America, North Mankato, MN.

# TABLE OF CONTENTS

LOST AT SEA.................................4

WHAT IS THE BERMUDA
    TRIANGLE?..............................8

IS THERE AN ANSWER?...............14

GLOSSARY................................22

TO LEARN MORE.....................23

INDEX.......................................24

# LOST AT SEA

A pilot takes off from a Florida airport. He flies toward the island of Bermuda. Suddenly, his **instruments** begin to fail.

The pilot calls **air traffic controllers** for help. But his radio cuts out. Soon his plane disappears from the **radar**. Is he lost in the Bermuda Triangle?

# WHAT IS THE BERMUDA TRIANGLE?

The Bermuda Triangle is an area of the Atlantic Ocean east of Florida. It stretches northeast to Bermuda and south to Puerto Rico. Many strange things have happened there.

## WHAT'S IN A NAME?

The Bermuda Triangle has many nicknames. Others include the Devil's Triangle and the Sea of Lost Ships.

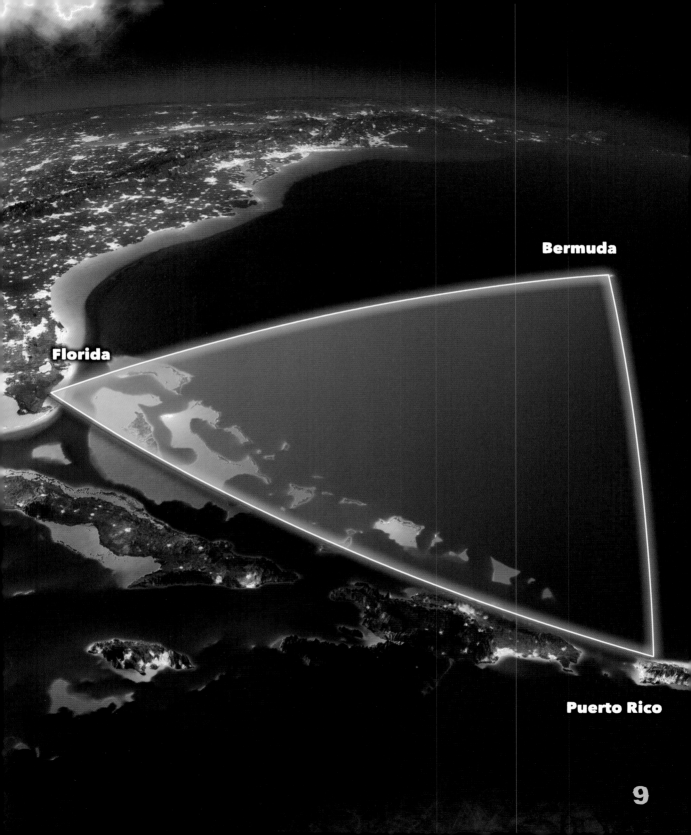

Bermuda

Florida

Puerto Rico

9

USS Cyclops

SAIL AWAY
The USS Cyclops is one of the most famous lost ships. It went missing with over 300 people on board.

Ships have disappeared in the Triangle for hundreds of years. **Ghost ships** have also been found in the area. They sail the sea with no crew.

Many planes have also been lost in the Triangle. Flight 19 is the most well-known disappearance. These five Navy planes **vanished** in 1945 during a training flight.

## HIDE AND SEEK

A rescue plane searched for Flight 19. It was never seen again.

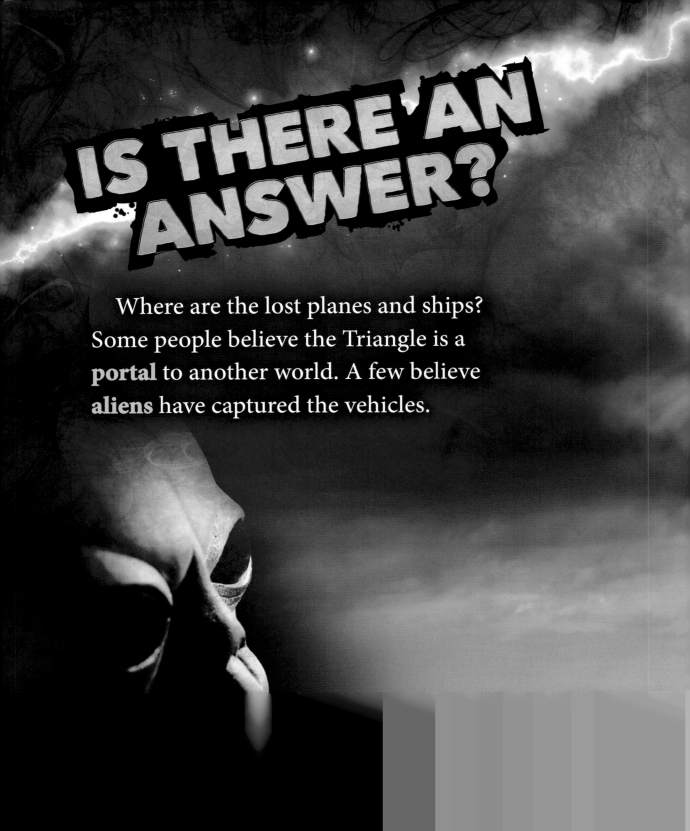

# IS THERE AN ANSWER?

Where are the lost planes and ships? Some people believe the Triangle is a **portal** to another world. A few believe **aliens** have captured the vehicles.

Many people look for simpler answers. Stormy weather could cause planes and ships to go down. Human error or **rogue waves** might also be to blame.

**Skeptics** think there is nothing mysterious about the Bermuda Triangle. Thousands of ships and planes travel there. Few have had problems.

# WALK THE PLANK

Pirates once sailed in the Bermuda Triangle. It is possible they sank some of the ships.

# FAMOUS DISAPPEARANCES

## Ellen Austin (1881)

The *Ellen Austin* finds a ghost ship. It sends a crew to sail it back to New York. The two ships are separated during a storm. When they meet again, there is no crew aboard the ghost ship. The *Ellen Austin* sends more of its crew to the ship. The ship disappears again.

## USS Cyclops (1918)

A U.S. Navy ship is lost on its way from Barbados to Maryland. A large crew and full load were on board.

## Flight 19 (1945)

Five Navy aircraft disappear in a training flight. A rescue plane also disappears while searching for the lost planes.

## Witchcraft (1967)

A boat sends a message to the Coast Guard after it hits an object. The Coast Guard searches but finds no sign of the vessel.

## Piper Navajo (1978)

An experienced pilot is close to landing in the Virgin Islands. Suddenly, his plane disappears from radar. Rescue searches are unable to find any pieces of the plane.

## Flight 201 (1984)

A small Cessna airplane slows and crashes into the ocean between Florida and the Bahamas. No sign of the plane is found.

We can only guess what has happened inside the Bermuda Triangle. Do pilots and sailors enter another world? Or are they victims of bad weather?

# GLOSSARY

**air traffic controllers**—people who monitor flight routes

**aliens**—beings from another planet

**ghost ships**—ships sailing the sea with no crew on board

**instruments**—the dials and controls on an airplane

**portal**—a doorway or gate

**radar**—a system of tracking aircraft in the air

**rogue waves**—large, unpredictable waves

**skeptics**—people who doubt the truth of something

**vanished**—disappeared suddenly

**victims**—people who are hurt or killed in a disaster

# TO LEARN MORE

## At the Library

Hawkins, John. *The World's Strangest Unexplained Mysteries*. New York, N.Y.: PowerKids Press, 2012.

Miller, Connie Colwell. *The Bermuda Triangle: The Unsolved Mystery*. Mankato, Minn.: Capstone Press, 2009.

Walker, Kathryn. *Mysteries of the Bermuda Triangle*. New York, N.Y.: Crabtree Pub., 2009.

## On the Web

Learning more about the Bermuda Triangle is as easy as 1, 2, 3.

1. Go to www.factsurfer.com.

2. Enter "Bermuda Triangle" into the search box.

3. Click the "Surf" button and you will see a list of related Web sites.

With factsurfer.com, finding more information is just a click away.

# INDEX

air traffic controllers, 6
aliens, 14
answers, 14, 17, 19
Atlantic Ocean, 8
Bermuda (islands), 4, 8, 9
Flight 19, 12, 13, 20
Florida, 4, 8, 9
ghost ships, 11
history, 11, 12, 13, 19, 20
instruments, 4
names, 8
Navy, 12
pilot, 4, 6, 21
pirates, 19
plane, 6, 12, 14, 17, 18
portal, 14

Puerto Rico, 8, 9
radar, 6
rogue waves, 17
sailors, 21
ships, 8, 11, 14, 17, 18, 19
skeptics, 18
USS *Cyclops*, 10, 11, 20
victims, 21
weather, 17, 21

The images in this book are reproduced through the courtesy of: Leigh Anne Meeks/ Algefoto, front cover (composite), p. 21 (composite); FeyginFoto, p. 4; Xavier Marchant/ Minerva Studio, pp. 4-5 (composite); Cultura Limited/ SuperStock, p. 6; Aleksander Mijatovic, pp. 6-7; Anton Balazh, p. 9; U.S. Naval Historical Center/ Wikipedia, pp. 10-11; Department of Defense/ Wikipedia, pp. 12-13, 13; photoBeard, p. 14; Nightman1965/ Minerva Studio, pp. 14-15 (composite); stoupa, p. 16; Pi-Lens, pp. 16-17; BioLife Pics.